Counting The Seasons

Heather E. Schwartz

Publishing Credits

Rachelle Cracchiolo, M.S.Ed., *Publisher*
Conni Medina, M.A.Ed., *Managing Editor*
Nika Fabienke, Ed.D., *Series Developer*
June Kikuchi, *Content Director*
John Leach, *Assistant Editor*
Kevin Pham, *Graphic Designer*

Image Credits: All images from from iStock and/or Shutterstock.

Library of Congress Cataloging-in-Publication Data

Names: Schwartz, Heather E., author.
Title: Counting : the seasons / Heather E. Schwartz.
Other titles: Seasons
Description: Huntington Beach, CA : Teacher Created Materials, [2018] | Audience: K to grade 3.
Identifiers: LCCN 2017026878 (print) | LCCN 2017029187 (ebook) | ISBN 9781425853297 (eBook) | ISBN 9781425849559 (pbk.)
Subjects: LCSH: Counting--Juvenile literature. | Seasons--Juvenile literature.
Classification: LCC QA113 (ebook) | LCC QA113 .S3925 2018 (print) | DDC 508.2--dc23
LC record available at https://lccn.loc.gov/2017026878

Teacher Created Materials
5301 Oceanus Drive
Huntington Beach, CA 92649-1030
http://www.tcmpub.com

ISBN 978-1-4258-4955-9

Printed in China 51497

Each year has four seasons.
They are **winter**, **spring**, **summer**, and **fall**.

Winter brings three months of cold. Build a snowman. Ride a sled.

Spring brings three months of warm sun.

Smell the flowers.
See them grow.

Summer brings three months of heat.
Play outside.
Ride a bike.

°C
°F
50
40
30
20
10
0
10
20
30
40
120
100
80
60
40
20
0
20
40

Fall brings three months of falling leaves.

Touch the leaves.
See the colors.

There are four seasons.
Each season is three months long.

summer
fall

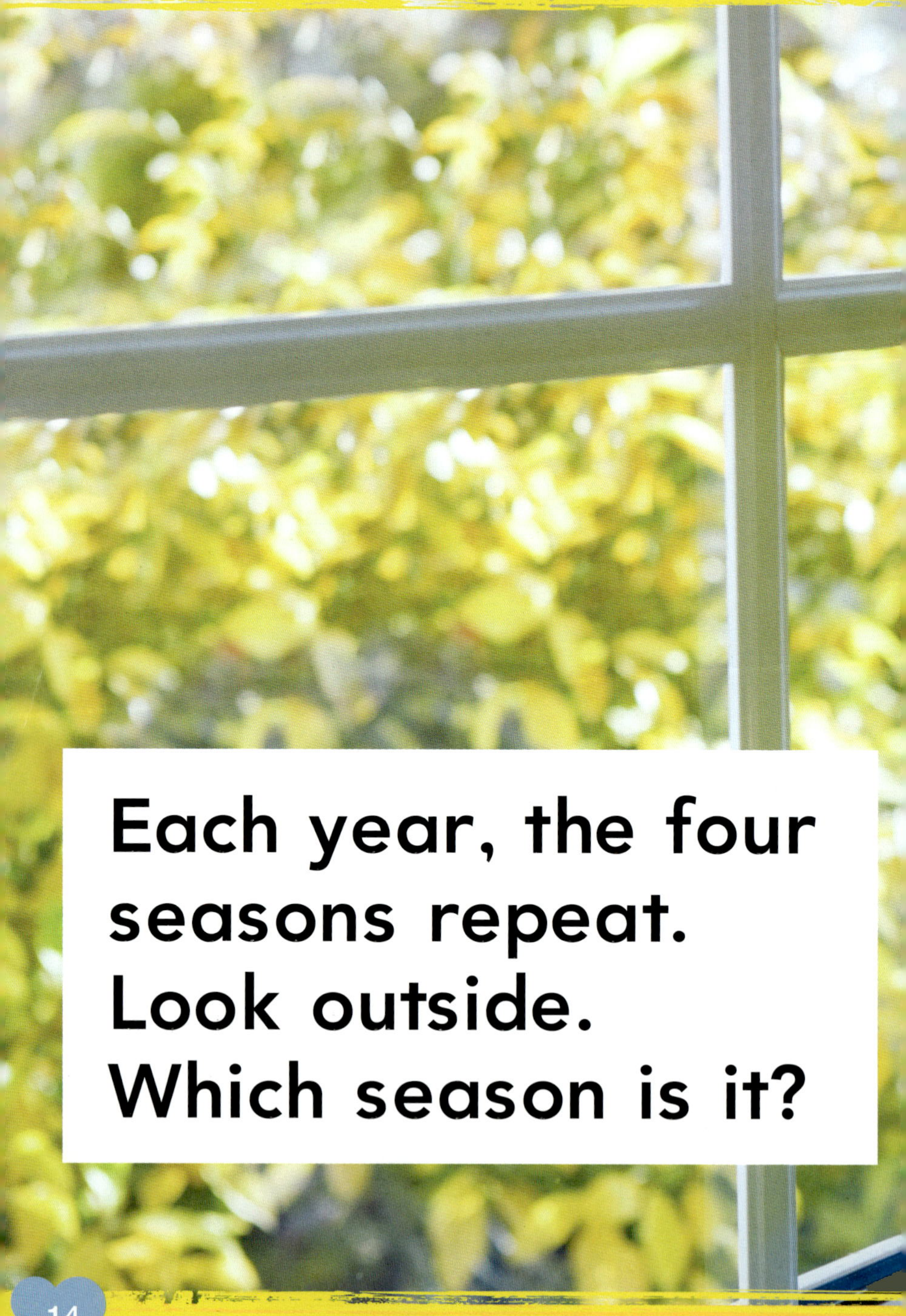

Each year, the four seasons repeat. Look outside. Which season is it?

Glossary

fall

spring

summer

winter